The Bravest Little Maccabee

By Chaia May

© 2016 LearningPlay Publications

Publisher
Editorial, Sales and Customer Service Office
LearningPlay Publications
Chaia May Education, LLC
Menlo Park, Ca 94025

©2016 All rights reserved.
No part of this material protected by this copyright notice may be reproduced or utilized in any form, electronic or mechanical, including photocopying, recording or by any information storage and retrieval system, without written permission from the copyright owner.

Library of Congress Cataloging-in-Publication Data
May, Chaia M. 1959-

Illustrated Children's Books:
ISBN   978-0-9864121-4-1
PCN   _____
1. Illustrated Children's Books, May

Illustrator: Samantha Geist
Cover Art by Samantha Geist, Age 9
Book Layout by Matt Weir Design
Photographs provided with permission by Josh and Liane

Join Us Online

Find us at LearningPlay.org. Look under "Publications" for this book and other early childhood books and media.

See our LearningPlay Facebook page too! Please feel free to comment and offer suggestions on the existing material as well as ideas for publications you would like to see in the future.

This book is dedicated to Maccabee and to all our
four-legged friends who teach us the
meaning of unconditional love.
- Joshua & Liane

To John, such a good man.
Your encouragement to share this story
along with your generous help
was truly inspirational.

Dear Readers,

This book is based on a true story of the life and death of Maccabee, a family's beloved dog. We hope it will help families deal not only with the loss of a cherished pet but also facilitate discussions that enable young children to cope with the death of anyone they love.

Readers have said that the story helped them prepare in anticipation of losing their pet by using the phrasing to explain to a young child that someone they love has passed away. I hope that this tale will also give parents courage to share their own feelings openly and create sacred moments around the rituals of loss. These moments may be the ones that the family will cherish most when they look back.

All we have is love and time. Love is boundless and limitless, Time, however, is finite. And like the beating of our hearts, we rarely notice it until we lose someone entirely and what we took for granted is gone. Each beat is precious and each moment it punctuates is fleeting. May every moment be a gift for the taking, and enrich the meaning of the word "present."

With love,
Chaia

A Bit About Chanukah

Chanukah, the Jewish Festival of Lights, commemorates courage and faith. It celebrates an unlikely military victory by a small band of Jewish men led by the Maccabee family. The oldest brother, Judah Maccabee, led a revolt for religious freedom in the second century B.C. against the Syrian-Greeks. He won with a clever strategy of waging battle at night, using his familiarity with the paths in his native town to his advantage.

The spiritual message of Chanukah is conveyed through a story in the Talmud (a body of Jewish civil law and tradition) which tells of a miracle that occurred after the Second Holy Temple in Jerusalem was ransacked. Afterwards, there was only enough oil for one day in the jar of oil which was needed to keep the *Ner Tamid,* (Eternal Light) in the Holy Temple continually lit. Miraculously, the oil lasted eight days allowing time to seek oil and replace it.

A *menorah* or candleholder typically has seven branches. A *Chanukiah* has eight branches, for the eight days of Chanukah. Chanukah literally means "dedication" as the Holy Temple was rededicated after it was desecrated and restored to it's holy or pure state. Traditionally the *chanukiah* has been put in the window to demonstrate with gratitude that we have religious freedom.

The Bravest Little Maccabee

Daddy walked in the door of his house with a suitcase and a hello to everyone just in time for Chanukah. Maccabee, their fluffy white dog, jumped up to greet him at the door. Maccabee kissed Daddy and made sure he was fine, just like every time Daddy came home from a business trip.

When Maccabee's cold nose touched Daddy's nose, also cold from having been out in the winter air, Daddy shook a little. Then he laughed to see Mac so happy to have him home.

However, the very next day, Maccabee didn't jump out of his bed to give everyone a good morning kiss as he usually did.

Mommy was concerned. She immediately made an appointment with the veterinarian.

"Does he have to get a shot?" asked Alexa, the youngest of the three sisters.

"I hope not!" she added.

"I don't know," said Mommy. "We will see. His name is Maccabee so I'm sure he will be a brave little dog."

After Mommy and Maccabee got home, Mommy sat down with her girls and said calmly, yet seriously, "Maccabee is sick. Sadly, he is not going to get better. He has cancer and the doctor does not know how long he will live. Let's say a prayer that he will be able to spend the whole Chanukah with us since he is a "Maccabee" and Chanukah is his holiday too!

At first the girls were very quiet. Then the middle sister, Chloe, asked Mommy a big question: "Is he going to be gone forever when he dies?"

"Yes" said Mommy. "But he will still live in our hearts. That's how we keep our loved ones close to us. We remember the sweet times we had together. Why don't you girls make a memory book of all the best times you have had with Maccabee?"

"Ok," said the girls. They got out their colored pens and pencils and drew pictures of when he made them laugh. Samantha, the oldest sister, remembered that Mac loved to eat paper. She chose to draw a picture of him playing innocent after he ate her homework not once but twice!

The sun was going down and it was officially the first night of Chanukah. They got out their *chanukiah* and were ready to light the candles.

Mommy said, "Samantha, would you please lead the prayers for Chanukah?"

"Can I add a special one for Maccabee?" Chloe asked.

"Of course you can," replied Mommy.

They all sang the prayers and ended with the song "*Sivivon, Sov, Sov, Sov.*" Little Alexa danced and turned. As they sang the words "*Nes gadol haya sham*" (A great miracle happened there), Chloe exclaimed, "Our prayer for Maccabee can be "*Nes katan haya po*!"

Chloe explained, "May a small miracle happen here--that our Maccabee can live for eight nights just like the oil lasted for eight nights in the Holy Temple."

Daddy smiled his approval and showed Chloe how to light the first candle with the *shamash*, the helper candle. The girls spun their dreidel, playing for pretzels and chocolate "*gelt*." Everyone sang funny verses to "The Dreidel Song" and opened a small gift. Then each girl gave Maccabee a get-well card. In return, Maccabee gave each girl a big, wet kiss. As he kissed them, he knocked down the spinning dreidel but they didn't care!

Dear Maccabee,

I love you so much and I will miss you so much. You're the best thing that ever happened to me. I will never meet a dog like you. I'm sorry that you can't stay with us for much longer but I will always remember you.

Love,
Sarantina

Dear Mickey I'm sorry that you are sick and you can't play with us or jump with us I love you
Love Alexa ♥

Hi, Maccabee I love you so, so, so, much you are the best Dog anybody cood have you are the best Dog in the world you will allways be in my hart
Love, Chloe

The next night they sang the traditional Chanukah prayer followed by *"Maoz Tzur"* while they lit the second candle. Samantha solemnly said, "Judah the Maccabee was the biggest and the bravest Maccabee but Maccabee is the smallest and the bravest one in our family!"

"Girls, you are all being very brave," said Daddy, while Mommy nodded in agreement.

He told them the story of how the Jews were also brave and managed to trick the soldiers to keep their Jewish traditions alive. They would take out a dreidel to play a special game with it every time the soldiers walked by. When the soldiers were gone they would bring out their holy books and learn from them.

That night, Maccabee wasn't able to jump up, but he was still wagging his tail. He rubbed noses with the girls and they gave him a pretzel treat from the winnings of their dreidel game.

The third night Maccabee couldn't walk around as much so the girls moved his bed to where they lit the candles and played. They gave him a special blanket as a present to keep him warm. He smiled and looked into their eyes. They were sure he was telling them how happy he was with their gift.

The fourth night they lit the candles and ate yummy potato *latkes* with applesauce and sour cream. Mommy said they could give Maccabee a treat. They gave him a piece of their *latkes*, which he ate happily. The girls sang the song "Oh Chanukah" and pretended to melt like candles. Once on the floor, they hugged Maccabee and held him tight.

The fifth and sixth nights the children made sure Maccabee was comfortable. They felt his breathing was slower and watched how he paid attention to the candles burning lower while flickering in and out. It was beautiful and sad. Still, they sang "Chanukah, Chanukah" and danced for him just as the lights seemed to dance; they were joyful at the miracle that Maccabee had made it through one more day and night and was still with them.

Everyone sat around the table and had *sufganiot*, the yummy jelly donuts that they eat in Israel on Chanukah. They told the story of how the small band of brave and smart Maccabees fought at night with bows and arrows against a huge army of soldiers riding on elephants. They won the battle because of Judah Maccabee and his clever strategy of fighting; he and his brothers knew every path inside and out while their enemies did not and lost their advantage.

On the seventh night of Chanukah, Maccabee was noticeably more tired. His breathing was heavy and it seemed like every breath was more of an effort.

With tears in her eyes and a waver in her voice, Samantha whispered, "Be brave, Maccabee, just like the clever widow Judith who was known for her beauty and bravery."

Mommy told the rest of the story: "When the spring water in their village was seized, Judith saved everyone by offering the enemy General a salty meal of cheese to make him thirsty. He was so thirsty that he drank too much wine. His soldiers fled in fear when they saw that she had slain him."

The eighth night of Chanukah came. The *chanukiah* lit the whole room with all its lights glowing brightly. Everyone felt it was a special night as they stood around the table and sang "*Mi Yimaleil.*" One by one, they put their arms around each other.

Alexa took Maccabee's paw and held that too. It was the last night and they were still together.

After a long silence, Daddy said, "*Nes katan haya po*: A small miracle happened here. Maccabee has made it through the eight nights of Chanukah." It was the best gift they could ever receive.

Very soon after, Mommy walked in the door after a long day at work to find a big surprise--Maccabee had gotten up from his pillow and was walking over to her to give her a kiss! With a grateful heart she murmured, "*Nes katan haya po.* This is another small miracle and a moment I will remember forever." A few hours later, Maccabee died.

The children were very sad yet grateful that they had gotten to spend all of Chanukah with Maccabee.

Mommy shared, "I believe Maccabee held on at the end for all of us to love him for as long as we could."

They waited until their deepest sadness had passed and their hearts were ready for a new pet to love. They also waited to show Maccabee respect and make it clear that no one could replace him.

When the family felt it was the right time, they got a puppy full of love and life. She filled their home with joy and a bit of chaos, spinning like a dreidel everywhere. She jumped on everyone all the time until they taught her proper doggy manners. They named the puppy "Latke" in the spirit of the holiday.

Every Chanukah after that, and in between of course, they remembered dear, sweet Maccabee -- the bravest little Maccabee that ever there was.

Dear Adults,

Children may have questions about why Maccabee got cancer and may fear that their parents or other loved ones will also get cancer and die. The best advice is to follow the lead of the child while being honest and hopeful in the broad sense of hope. "I hope they will heal" if it is not a terminal illness, for example. For the others who are likely not to heal, the children may want to say "I hope they aren't in pain." You can reassure them by saying, "It is very rare for people and animals to die young and that most people and animals die when they get old." Maccabee was ten years old, or seventy in people years.

Children are naturally spiritual. They can be reminded to find the sacred in small things. Making a pet's last days more comfortable by surrounding him or her with loving acts of kindness is known in Judaism as a "mitzvah." It is one of many deeds from the Jewish tradition that even very young children can perform. The mitzvah of being by the bedside of a loved one who is sick is very significant. The teachings say that because it could extend or save the life of a person, or in this case, a beloved animal, it is one of the most redeeming of Jewish ethical obligations.

Lastly, fear can be seen as the opposite of love. Worry or fear "pinches" off love, so emphasizing how we can cherish someone rather than worry about him or her allows us and them somewhere to put our emotional energy.

Glossary

Chanukah: Literally means "Dedication," referring to the re-dedication of the Holy Temple after it was desecrated. This winter holiday lasts eight nights and families typically celebrate by lighting candles, playing dreidel and eating foods fried in oil.

Chanukiah: A candleholder with nine branches used to light candles for Chanukah.

Dreidel: A spinning top with the Hebrew letters "Nun," "Gimmel," "Hey," and "Shin." These are the first letters of the Hebrew phrase, "Nes gadol haya sham," a great miracle happened here.

Dreidel Game: Children sit together in a circle and each gets a piece of gelt or coin to put in the middle. They take turns spinning the dreidel and play for a reward of pretzels, coins or chocolates. The rules are:
Nun= get none, Gimmel = get all, Hey = get half, and Shin = put one in.

Gelt: Money. At Chanukah chocolate coins wrapped in foil are used as substitutes for real gelt in the dreidel game.

Latkes: Potato pancakes fried in oil, considered traditional holiday fare. They are usually topped with applesauce and sour cream.

Judah Maccabee: The oldest of five brothers of the Maccabee family. He led the revolt against the Syrian-Greeks for the province of Judea.

Judith the Widow: A brave widow who saved the Jewish people in her village by tricking and slaying General Holofernes which scared his army away.

Maccabees: The heroes of the Chanukah story.

Menorah: A candelabrum with seven branches found in the Holy Temple of Jerusalem. It is a symbol of the Jewish people and the State of Jerusalem. It is found on the Israeli flag.

Mitzvah (Plural: Mitzvot): One of the 613 commandments in the Torah. Loosely translated as good deeds.

Nes Gadol Haya Po: A great miracle happened here.
Nes Gadol Haya Sham: A great miracle happened there.

Shamash (Helper Candle): The candle on the chanukiah used to light the other candles on Chanukah.

Sufganiyot: Jelly donuts, eaten traditionally for Chanukah in Israel.

Chanukah, Chanukah

Chanukah, Chanukah
Chag yafeh kol kach
Ohr chaviv, mi-saviv
Gil li-yeled rach.

Chanukah, Chanukah
Sivivon, sov, sov
Sov, sov, sov! Sov, sov, sov!
Ma nayim vi-tov.

Chanukah Oh Chanukah

Oh Chanukah, Oh Chanukah
Come light the menorah
Let's have a party
We'll all dance the horah
Gather 'round the table
We'll give you a treat
Dreidels to play with
And latkes to eat.
And while we
Are playing
The candles are burning low
One for each night
They shed a sweet light
To remind us of days long ago.

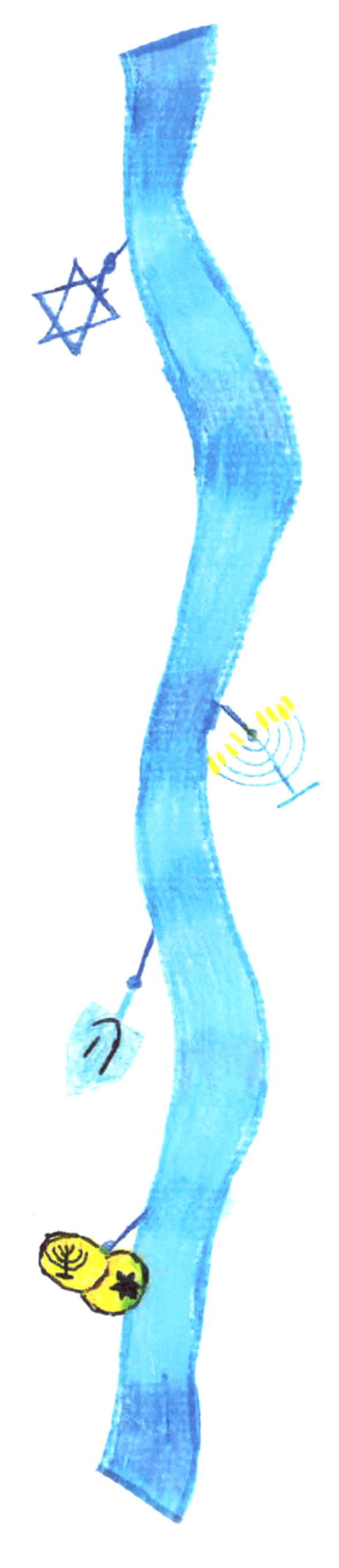

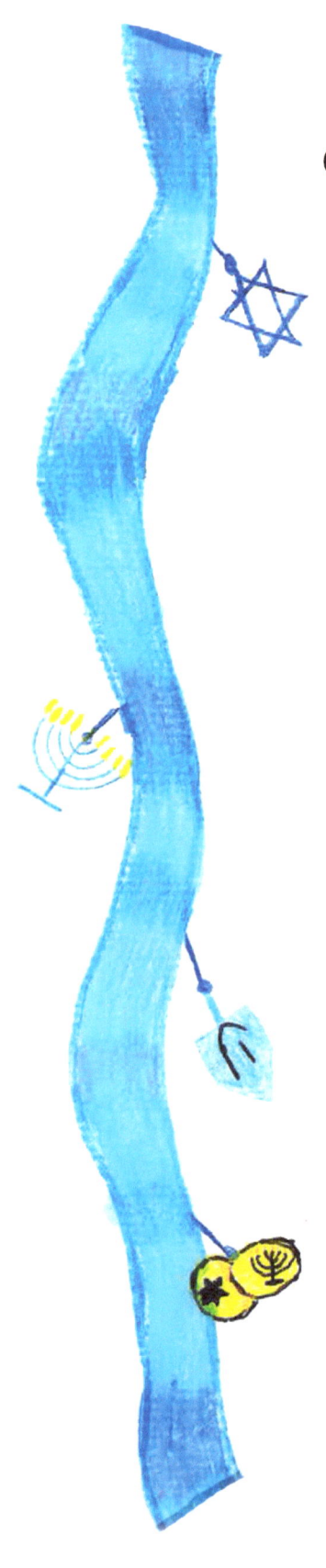

Yiddish Lyrics:

Oy Chanukah oy Chanukah, a yontif a sheiner
A lustiker a freylicher nito noch a zeyner
Alle nacht in dreydlech shpiln mir
Zudik hesse latkes essen mir
Geshvinder tsindt kinder
di Chanukah lichtelech on
Zol yeder bazunder bazingen dem vunder
un tantzen freylech in kohn (2x)

or:

Oy Chanukah oy Chanukah
A yontif a shayner,
A lustiker a freylekher
Nisht do nokh azoyner
Ale nakht mit dreidlech shpiln mir,
Frishe heise latkes, esn on a shir.
Geshvinder, tsindt kinder
Di Chanukah likhtlech on,
Zogt "Al Hanisim", loybt Got far di nisim,
Un lomir ale tantsen in kon.
Zogt "Al Hanisim", loybt Got far di nisim,
Lomir ale tantsen tsuzamen.

Dreidel, Dreidel

I have a little dreidel
I made it out of clay
And when it's dry and ready
Then dreidel I shall play!

Chorus:
Oh dreidel, dreidel, dreidel
I made it out of clay
And when it's dry and ready
Then dreidel I shall play!

It has a lovely body
With legs so short and thin
And when my dreidel's tired
It drops and then I win!

(Chorus)

My dreidel's always playful
It loves to dance and spin
A happy game of dreidel
Come play now, let's begin!

(Chorus)

I have a little dreidle
I made it out of plastic
I know it's not traditional
but I think it's fantastic

(Chorus)

I have a little dreidle
I made it out of chocolate.
When I went to spin it
it had melted in my pocket

(Chorus)

Maoz Tzur

Ma'oz tzur yeshu'ati,
lecha na'eh leshabe'ach,
tikon beit tefilati,
vesham todah nezabe'ach.
Le'et tachin matbe'ach
mitzar hamenabe'ach.
Az egmor
beshir mizmor
chanukat hamizbe'ach

English Translation:

My refuge, my rock of salvation!
It is a pleasure to sing Your praises.
Let our house of prayer be restored.
And there we will offer You our thanks.
When You will have prepared the slaughter
Of the the barking foe,
Then we will celebrate with song and psalm
The dedication of the altar.

Mi Y'maleil

Mi y'maleil g'vurot Yisraeil?
Otan mi yimneh?
Hein b'chol dor yakum hagibor
go-eil ha-am

Who can retell the things that befell us?
Who can count them?
In ev'ry age
a hero or sage came to our aid (repeat)

Sh'ma! Bayamim ha-heim
bazman hazeh
Makabi moshia ufodeh
Uv-yaminu kol am Yisraeil,
yit-acheid yakum l'hi-ga-eil.

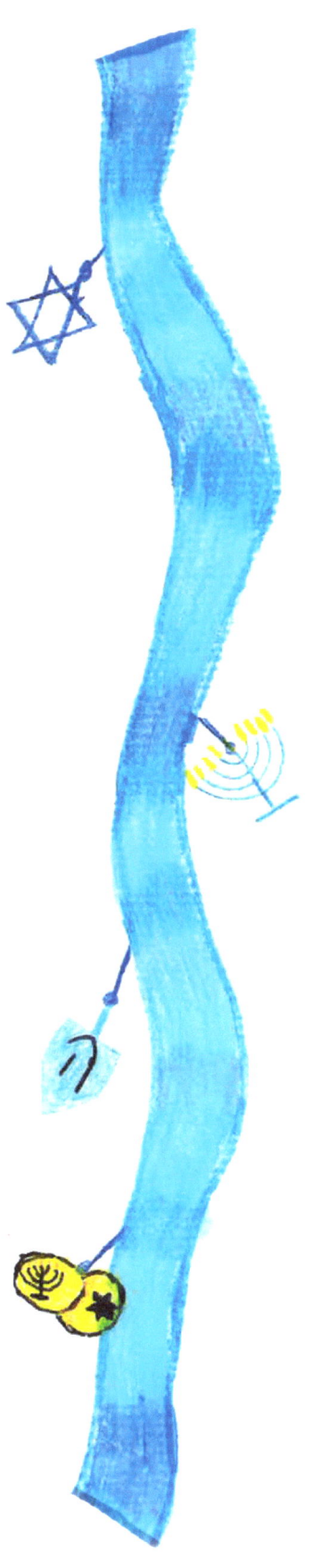

Sivivon Sov Sov Sov

Sivivon, sov, sov, sov
Chanukah, hu chag tov
Chanukah, hu chag tov Sivivon, sov, sov, sov!

Chag simcha hu la-am
Nes gadol haya sham
Nes gadol haya sham
Chag simcha hu la-am.

(Translation)

Dreidel, spin, spin, spin.
Chanukah is a great holiday.
It is a celebration for our nation.
A great miracle happened there.

For music, see:
Hebrewsongs.com from Jewishworldlife.com
or
songsforteaching.com

Candles are added to the hanukkiyah (menorah) from right to left but are kindled from left to right.

The newest candle is lit first. (On the Shabbat of Hanukkah, kindle the Hanukkah lights first and then the Shabbat candles.)

Light the shamash (the helper candle) first, using it to kindle the rest of the Hanukkah lights.

As you do, say or sing:

Baruch atah, Adonai Eloheinu, Melech haolam, asher kid'shanu b'mitzvotav v'tsivanu l'hadlik ner shel Hanukkah.

Blessed are You, Adonai our God, Sovereign of all, who hallows us with mitzvot, commanding us to kindle the Hanukkah lights.

Baruch atah, Adonai Eloheinu, Melech haolam, she-asah nisim laavoteinu v'imoteinu bayamim hahaeim baz'man hazeh.

Blessed are You, Adonai our God, Sovereign of all, who performed wonderous deeds for our ancestors in days of old at this season.

For first night only:

Baruch atah, Adonai Eloheinu, Melech haolam, shehecheyanu v'kiy'manu v'higianu laz'man hazeh.

Blessed are You, Adonai our God, Sovereign of all, for giving us life, for sustaining us, and for enabling us to reach this season.

Hanerot Halalu
We kindle these lights because of the wondrous deliverance You performed for our ancestors. During these eight days of Hanukkah, these lights are sacred; we are not to use them but only to behold them, so that their glow may rouse us to give thanks for Your wondrous acts of deliverance.

Chanukah Candle Lighting Prayers

One candle is added to the menorah each night. The first night, you light only the shammus (usually the the highest candle) and one Chanukkah candle. By the eighth night, you light all of the candles.

Candles should be added to the menorah from right to left (like Hebrew writing). The shammus candle is lit first. While holding the shammus candle, recite the following blessings.

בָּרוּךְ אַתָּה יְיָ אֱלֹהֵינוּ מֶלֶךְ הָעוֹלָם
אֲשֶׁר קִדְּשָׁנוּ בְּמִצְוֹתָיו וְצִוָּנוּ
לְהַדְלִיק נֵר שֶׁל חֲנֻכָּה: (אָמֵן)

Blessed are you, Lord, our God, sovereign of the universe
Who has sanctified us with His commandments and commanded us
to light the lights of Chanukkah. (Amen)

Barukh atah Adonai, Eloheinu, melekh ha'olam
asher kidishanu b'mitz'votav v'tzivanu
l'had'lik neir shel Chanukah. (Amein)

בָּרוּךְ אַתָּה יְיָ אֱלֹהֵינוּ מֶלֶךְ הָעוֹלָם
שֶׁעָשָׂה נִסִּים לַאֲבוֹתֵינוּ בַּיָּמִים הָהֵם בַּזְּמַן הַזֶּה: (אָמֵן)

Blessed are you, Lord, our God, sovereign of the universe
Who performed miracles for our ancestors in those days at this time. (Amen)

Barukh atah Adonai, Eloheinu, melekh ha'olam
she'asah nisim la'avoteinu bayamim haheim baziman hazeh. (Amein)

This prayer is said on the first night only.

בָּרוּךְ אַתָּה יְיָ אֱלֹהֵינוּ מֶלֶךְ הָעוֹלָם
שֶׁהֶחֱיָנוּ וְקִיְּמָנוּ וְהִגִּיעָנוּ לַזְּמַן הַזֶּה: (אָמֵן)

Blessed are you, Lord, our God, sovereign of the universe
who has kept us alive, sustained us, and enabled us to reach this season (Amen)

Barukh atah Adonai, Eloheinu, melekh ha'olam
shehecheyanu v'kiyimanu v'higi'anu laz'man hazeh. (Amein)

Chaia May is a writer, musician, storyteller and educator living in the Bay Area. She holds a B.A. from Wellesley College, an M.A from Stanford University and has extensive post-graduate work in Early Childhood. Chaia has written a series of Jewish Hands-On Holiday books for parents and teachers as well as a Pre-Kindergarten math picture book series. Chaia uses humor and stories to make concepts accessible to young children.

She is delighted to share her series of books on her website: **LearningPlay.org.**

Samantha Geist was born in Toronto, Canada. She now lives in California with her mum, dad, two sisters and new puppy. Having taken art classes since the age of four, she has truly developed a love and gift for art. Samantha drew Maccabee's cover portrait at nine years old with chalk pastels and colored pencils. In her spare time, Samantha enjoys dancing, reading, biking and baking.

Maccabee is a Coton de Toulear. He looked like a stuffed animal at eight weeks old when he arrived and then lived happily with his new family for ten years. May he rest in peace.

www.ingramcontent.com/pod-product-compliance
Lightning Source LLC
Chambersburg PA
CBHW041537040426
42446CB00002B/125